ACRYLIC AND DIPPING POWDER
Product Knowledge and Applications

TABLE OF CONTENTS

ABOUT THE AUTHOR

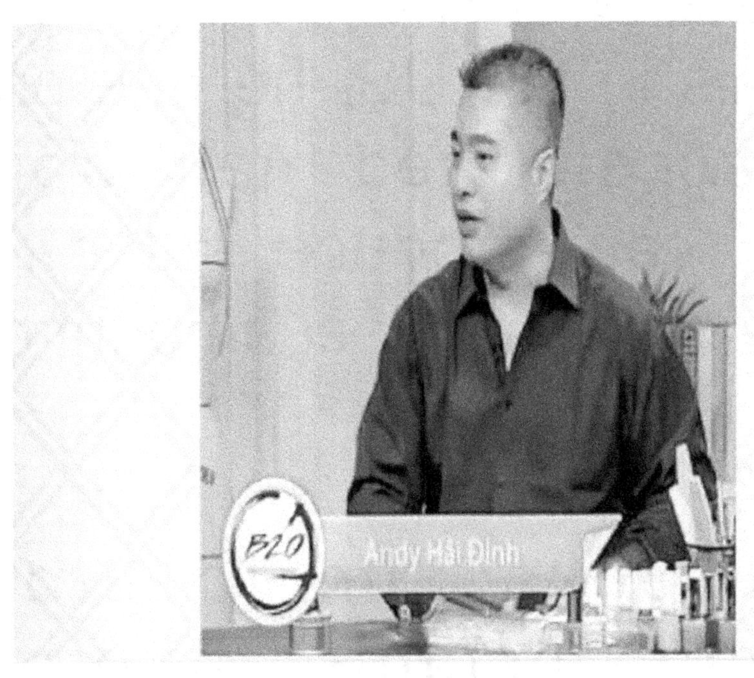

Andy Hai Dinh is an established nail artist, educator, market researcher, and salon business consultant who has been active in the US beauty industry since 2004. His nail works have gained more than 2.8 million views on Google and 23k followers on Instagram (@andyhaidinh).

As a former brand ambassador for some of the most prestigious international nail brands and after training over 1600 nail professionals in the US, he has proven that his accelerated nail training curriculum can produce salon-ready technicians in the shortest amount of time.

Andy's books aim to provide fundamental insights of product knowledge, application procedures, nail art and business knowledge which all nail professionals and salon owners should master.

Andy Hai Dinh is the founder of LONA (Life of Nails Academy) - an online platform for nail training courses and nail resources. He is also a trader profiting from swing trading stocks and Forex currencies.

ACCELERATED ONLINE NAIL TRAINING COURSES & BOOKS AT:

www.pensight.com/x/lona

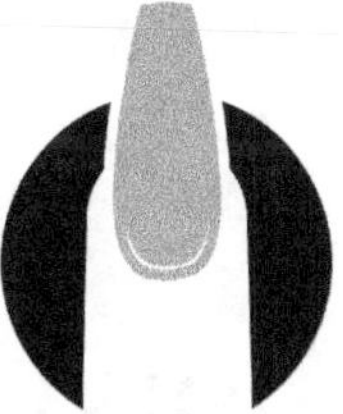

Life Of Nails Academy

Nail Your Future!

INTRODUCTION

Thank you for purchasing my book. This comprehensive manual is the accumulation of product knowledge and basic application procedures for acrylic nails and dipping powder nails.

This book also covers nail terminology, tips and troubleshooting methods for common nail problems you may encounter when working with your clients.

As nail professionals, we should have an in-depth understanding of our trade so that we can safely provide services, fulfill the needs of our clients and answer any question within the spectrum of our practice.

I truly hope this book will assist you to achieve the skills, the confidence and the pride of being a proud nail slayer.

Andy Hai Dinh

ACRYLIC CHEMISTRY - TERMS AND DEFINITIONS

There are three main types of acrylic primer:

1. ACID-BASED:

•They can cause the enhancement to yellow if not used properly. If the primer touches the existing product during a fill in, back fill, refill or rebalance, it could cause yellowing. Applying product over wet primer will surely cause yellowing.

•It is corrosive to human skin. In 2001, the Consumer Products Safety Commission began requiring that all products containing more than 5% methacrylic acid be packaged in a child proof container.

•Acid-based were the original primers used in the nail industry. They contain between 30 - 100% methacrylic acid and are a safety net that nail technicians have used for many years to promote adhesion.

•It is very important to use extreme care with acid-based primers. When applying, it should be used sparingly. Just dot it on the natural nail, doing 5 nails at a time before putting brush back into bottle. Be cognizant of NOT touching any surrounding soft tissue with the primer. When it comes to acid-based primers, less is best.

2. NON-ACID:

Non-acid primers actually do contain acid; just not methacrylic acid. They will not burn the skin; although prolonged, repeated contact with any chemical must be avoided to prevent an adverse skin reaction. This type of primer is used to make the natural nail more compatible with the enhancement product. It chemically bonds the
same way as an acid- based primer.

3. ACID-FREE:

Acid-free primer is the newest kid on the block and does not contain any acid components. When used properly, these primers are equal to that of a primer containing methacrylic acid and are superior to a nonacid primer. Acid-free primers will not discolor the enhancement nor will they burn the skin. Unlike acid-based primers, acid-free primers should be applied liberally to achieve excellent adhesion.

POLYMER:

These are long chemical chains (can be liquid, but normally solid). The chemical reaction that creates a polymer is called polymerization. Polymers also contain initiators and color. Polymer is often referred to as "powder ".

INITIATOR:

This starts the chemical reaction. In acrylic, it is BENZOYL PEROXIDE inside the powder molecule that initiates the chemical reaction between the powder and liquid.

COLOR:

TITANIUM DIOXIDE is the ingredient that controls the pigment and opaque nature of acrylic.

TYPES OF POLYMERS

HOMO-POLYMER:

Single type of polymer (NOTE: pure Ethyl Methacrylate makes a faster set).

CO-POLYMER:

Two types of polymers are used to create a polymer chain (NOTE: adding Methyl Methacrylate slows the curing time).

MONOMER:

Is one molecule that can join with others and create polymer chains. This is normally in the liquid form. Monomer contains color stabilizers and additional plasticizers. Monomer is often referred to as "liquid".

DEHYDRATOR:

The dehydrator removes moisture and pH balances the nail plate. This creates a dry surface for improved adhesion and action of the primers.

STAGES OF ACRYLIC

All acrylic products have different stages they go through. In understanding these stages, it will give you an insight on different systems you use. Knowing the stages of your particular system gives you information needed to help you master applications more proficiently.

1. WET STAGE:

When the powder and liquid first interact until the product turns into a solid matter. The time can be anywhere from 10-15 seconds depending on the temperature variations.

2. WORKING STAGE:

When the acrylic product is a solid gel like matter which is pliable and easily moved around with a brush. Your time to work with the product is anywhere from 30 seconds to 1 minute and 30 seconds. The brush will be used to its full potential at this point in application. Use the brush to spread, push, pull and even out the acrylic throughout the nail, setting the product in its final position before hardening.

3. MOLDING STAGE:

All products have this stage but, in some cases, the 'molding stage' is overlooked because it is very brief. The product at this point is a solid matter and can no longer be moved around with the brush. Molding Stage times will vary from product to product. You will have more molding time with products that have a shorter wet stage and working stage and less molding time with products that have a longer wet and working stage. For fast setting products the molding stage can be anywhere from 2 ½ minutes to 5 minutes. For the slower set products, the molding stage can be anywhere from 2 to 4 minutes. By shaping and molding the product this will create a better C-Curve which helps the overall structure of the nail.

4. CURING STAGE:

This is when the product starts to turn into a hard plastic. With either a fast or slow product your curing (hardening) time is about the same. From the time you start to form the nail until the time it is fully hardened is approximately 6-7 minutes. When the acrylic is no longer pliable to mold or shape is when the curing stage starts. To check when the nail is ready to start filing, take your brush handle and tap the top of the nail. You want to hear a sharp and crisp clicking sound before you start to file.

www.pensight.com/x/lona

ACRYLIC POWDERS

Acrylic Powders combine the latest technology in chemical composition of cross-linked polymers that result in an ultimate scratch resistant surface providing clients the durability they demand. The powders also include color stabilizers to ensure color stability and coupled with advanced polymer chemistry, it allows the technician complete control over product placement while providing self-leveling capabilities for each application.

FEATURES & BENEFITS:

Most acrylic systems have a cross-linked chemistry of polymers that creates the additionalstrength and durability needed for professional results. This formulated blend also gives the acrylic the flexibility clients demand. Allowstechnicians to achieve a super fine finish with minimal filing. Advanced color stabilizers ensure no yellowing or discoloration of the acrylic.

DIRECTIONS:

Combine your choice of Acrylic Powder and Liquid to create strong beautiful nails. Acrylic application procedures incorporate an easy press and pull method giving you total control of the product. Dip brush into liquid and then into powder to create a ball (2:1 ratio). Form nail.

•COVER ACRYLICS:

An acrylic powder that offers more opaque nail coverage than the traditional pink acrylic powder. These powders are ideal for providing flawless looking nails that compliment a variety of skin tones and creating great ombre blends.

FEATURES:

For use in creating nail extensions, masking imperfections, discolorations & fill lines.

•GLOW IN THE DARK ACRYLIC POWDER:

Containing glow pigments to create nails with solid color by day and transform to emit an eye-catching luminous glow at night.

FEATURES:

Works with any liquid monomer. Glow charges with any light source or UV light exposure.

•NEON ACRYLIC POWDER:

Containing neon color pigments to create neon color nails.

FEATURES:

Works with any liquid monomer. Glow in UV light exposure.

•GLITTER ACRYLIC POWDER:

Clear powder mixed with sparkling loose glitter.

•SHIMMER ACRYLIC POWDER:

Solid color mixed with very fine glitter particles.

•JELLY ACRYLIC POWDER:

Sheer color powders.

EMA monomer is designed to combine easy application with superior adhesion in combination with acrylic powders. The traditional set time allows for extended workability and maximum product control. EMA liquid has a lower odor than most traditional MMA acrylic liquids and offers a superior working blend with any acrylic powders for a smooth application while staying pliable to allow the technician the working time necessary to perfect their nail prior to filing.

FEATURES & BENEFITS:

EMA monomers are Ethyl Methacrylate based liquid with chemical stabilizer to deter chemical sensitivity. It is a no MMA formula. The traditional set time allows for extended workability and maximum product control. The combination of the cross-link polymer with the flexibility of EMA liquid gives the nails additional strength. Acrylic nails created with EMA liquid will not crystallize. The combination of powder and EMA liquid is a stable chemical reaction not influenced by outside temperature or liquid to powder ratios that cause 20crystallization. EMA liquid normally is formulated with self-leveling stabilizers that will allow technicians to apply the products thinner, smoother and faster.

DIRECTIONS: Combine your choice of EMA monomer and powder to create strong beautiful nails. The recommended combination of liquid to powder is 2:1. However, product ratios can vary due to temperature variation in the work area. Due to the chemical make-up, strength and wear-ability are not compromised.

DIPPING ACRYLIC CHEMISTRY

Understanding Acrylic Dipping System:

1. Dip acrylic coating is formed by the cyanoacrylate (glue base) dissolving the dipping powder.

2. Particle size of the dipping powders is processed further to remove larger particles from traditional acrylic powder.

3. The activator in the system accelerates the curing/hardening process - without it, it would take hours for the base and finish glue to cure/harden.

4. Dipping acrylics are more durable than nail polish, gel polish, and other types of soak-off gels. They remove easily with acetone and will not cause nail thinning as the cyanoacrylate in
the base and top coats breaks up easily. The system has superior adhesion which makes lifting less common than other nail enhancements. Nails become stronger underneath due to the protection dipping acrylics provide as well as the formulation which contains vitamins and no methacrylate which soften the nail beds.

1. Prep Solution (bottle #1):

Removes moisture and oil from the nail surface to improve adhesion. Cleanses and sanitizes the nail surface by eliminating traces of bacteria. Prep can be used with any other artificial product system.

FEATURES & BENEFITS:

Sanitizes nail surface. Prepares nails for nail enhancements. Prevents lifting.

DIRECTIONS:

Apply one coat to all ten nails and allow to dry. Follow with Dip Base (bottle #2).

2. Dip Base (bottle #2):

Self leveling resin with medium viscosity. Formulated to adhere to the natural nail plate and to absorb the right amount of acrylic dipping powder. The base glue is slower drying than the top glue and has more flexibility.

FEATURES & BENEFITS:

Medium viscosity for even coverage. Fast-drying. Easily dissolved in Acetone.

No Ethyl Methacrylate, HPMA, HEMA, or TFEMA.

DIRECTIONS:

Apply one coat to the entire nail and dip into desired color of acrylic dipping powder and dust off excess. Repeat above step and follow with Activator (bottle #3). To maintain easy opening, clean neck of bottle with Acetone. Do not get solvent in bottle.

3. Activator (bottle #3):

This brush-on activator in essence is a glue drying solution which will help set your acrylic dipping powder nails and make them long-lasting and strong.

FEATURES & BENEFITS:

"Cures" the dip enhancement in approximately 60 to 90 seconds. Makes the dip nail enhancements strong and durable.

DIRECTIONS:

Apply a generous coat to all ten nails and allow to dry. File and shape the nails and apply another thin and even coat of Activator and allow to dry. Follow with 2 coats of Glue Top (bottle #4) to finish or, depending on preference, with 1 coat of LED/UV No-Cleanse Gel Top Coat and cure for 1.5 minutes in LED/

UV gel lamp. If using gel top coat, only apply the Activator #3 once prior to filing, and buffing.

4. Glue Top (bottle #4):

An air dry, self-leveling top coat, that seals and protects the dip nail enhancement giving it an even, glossy finish. It is thinner and dries faster than the base due to the high shine effect.

FEATURES & BENEFITS:

Fast and air drying. Durable and glossy finish.

DIRECTIONS:

Apply one coat to each nail of one hand and immediately apply a second coat on same hand. Repeat the above step on the other hand. To maintain easy opening, clean neck of bottle with Acetone. Do not get solvent in bottle.

•LED/UV No-Cleanse Top Gel:

A no-cleanse, light-activated gel that is the perfect finishing step for extremely glossy and durable nails.

FEATURES & BENEFITS:

LED & UV Curable. No cleanse, no buffing top coat. No chipping, spiking or pitting. Non-yellowing with a mirror finish.

CURE TIME:

LED 90 seconds, UV 3 minutes.

DIRECTIONS:

Use over gel polish, acrylic or dipping powder to seal and protect. Do not buff nail smooth. Apply a thin layer of LED/UV Top Gel making sure to cap the free edge. Cure for 90 seconds under LED lamp or cure for 3 minutes under UV lamp. Keep capped when not in use.

•Cuticle Oil:

Light and non-greasy, hydrates dry and damaged cuticles to promote healthy nail growth.

FEATURES & BENEFITS:

Subtle scent that won't interfere with spa services. Thinner viscosity to absorb into the skin faster. Works with natural nails or artificial nails.

DIRECTIONS:

Apply a small amount of Cuticle Oil to the cuticle area and the skin surrounding the nail.

•Nail Primer:

Formulated to penetrate the nail, releasing moisture and oil in preparation for nail enhancements. Creates a perfectly dry working surface, assuring maximum adhesion of enhancements with no pop-offs or lifting.

FEATURES & BENEFITS:

Consists of Methacrylic Acid. Promotes adhesion. Can be used with any artificial product.

DIRECTIONS:

Apply 2 coats of Nail Primer sparingly to the natural nail surface. Do not let the primer flow on the cuticle or the skin. Once the primer is dry, you will notice a chalky white appearance. If primer is spilled, rinse thoroughly with water and neutralize the burn with an alcohol-based product.

•Nail Glue:

A medium viscosity glue that is designed for simple tip applications or nail repairs. Designed for all types of tip applications.

FEATURES & BENEFITS:

Fast drying. Easy nozzle-type applicator offers smooth flow dispensing. Medium viscosity and will not crystallize.

DIRECTIONS:

For tip application, apply minimal amount to Contact Point of the tip (the well of the tip) and rock tip on nail to eliminate air pockets.

•Pure Acetone:

Used to remove acrylics, dipping powder and gel polish. Can be used to cleanse oil traces and dehydrate the natural nail plates.

•LED/UV Matte Gel Top Coat:

Gives nails a modern, trendy matte finish when applied over any powder or gel polish color.

FEATURES & BENEFITS:

Reinvents any color to create a matte effect. Endless design opportunities. LED/UV Curable.

DIRECTIONS:

Apply on top of Gel Polish, Dipping Powder or Acrylic Nails for an all-over matte finish. Cure UV for 2 minutes or LED for 60 sec.

NATURAL-NAIL PREPARATION PROCEDURE

Proper preparation of the nail plate determines how the artificial nail is going to wear between maintenance appointments. It helps eliminate lifting and peeling of the artificial nail. Complete removal of the non-living tissue, skin surrounding the perimeter of the nail plate, sometimes not visible to the naked eye, will ensure successful long-term wear of the artificial nail.
Begin all nail services by having client wash their hands with soap and water and apply hand sanitizer. Technician

should also wash and sanitize prior to service.

Step #1 - Gently Push Back the Cuticle, using the spoon end of a pusher.

Step #2 - Remove the non-living tissue carefully from the nail plate using the non-living tissue remover end of a pusher.

Step #3 - Remove the shine from the nail plate using a 180Grit or a fine paper sanding band with electric file at 4k RPM by filing in one direction from cuticle to free edge.

Step #4 - Remove the filing dust from the nail plate using a Cleansing Wipe.

Step #5 - Apply Nail Prep Solution to the natural nail to cleanse and dehydrate the surface of the nail. Apply Primer if necessary.

NAIL TIP APPLICATION

Step #1 - Size the tip that best fits the nail securely from nail groove to nail groove.

Step #2 - Sparingly apply nail glue to the well of the tip and gently rock the tip onto the nail from the free-edge pushing down toward the cuticle. This will eliminate air pockets.

Step #3 - Cut the tip to the desired length using tip cutters or scissors.

Step #4 - Using a fine paper sanding band and electric file at 6k RPM to blend the tip to the natural nail. Pre-thin the remainder of the tip for optimum pinching capability and to ensure proper adhesion

NOTE: Do not perform tip blending on white-color plastic tips (French plastic tips).

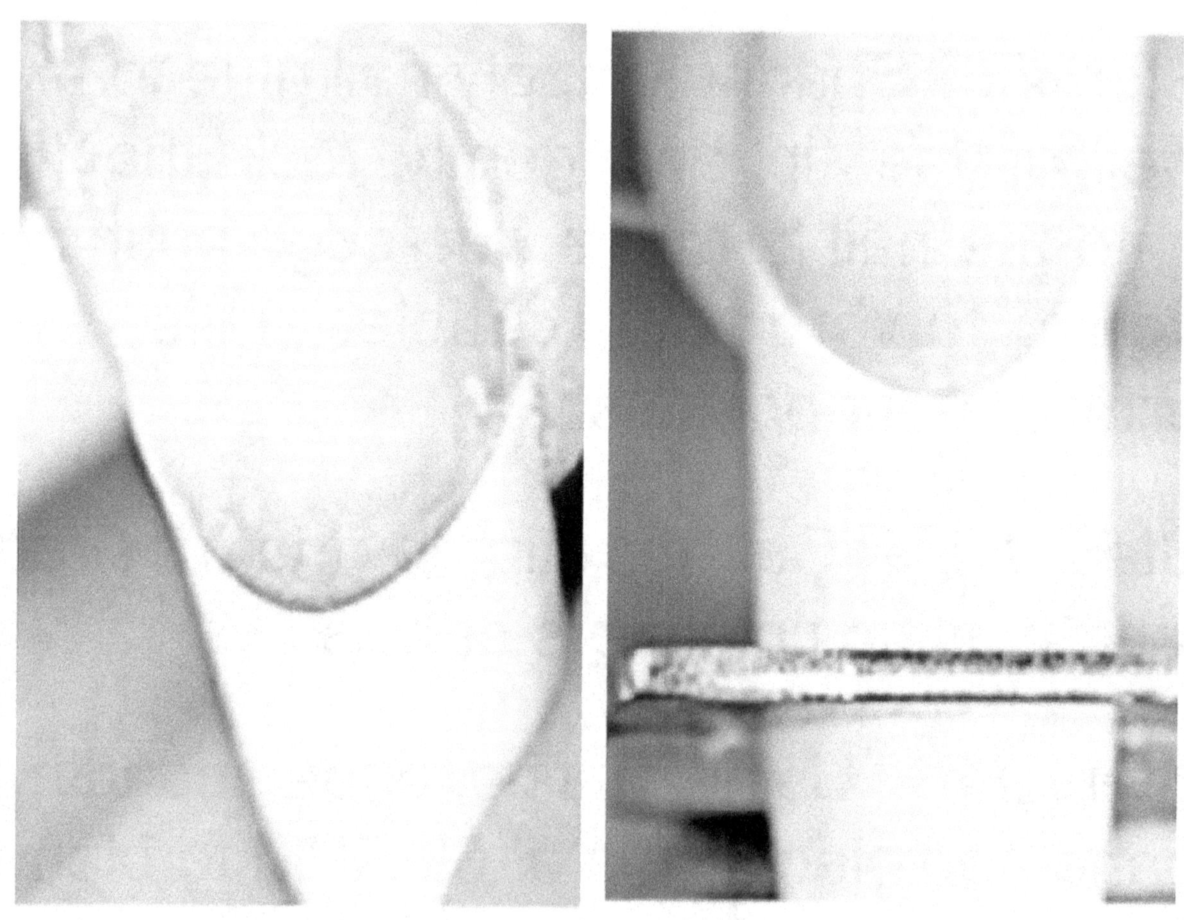

Use 100/100 Grit Nail File.

PRELIMINARY SHAPING:

1. Free Edge: Keep file straight, use lots of support. This is to start the basic shape of the nail. Turn hand around, to achieve hard square ensure file is perpendicular to free edge.

2. Side Walls: Lock elbow to side. Keeping the file parallel with the finger and the round end of file towards the

client, remove any excess bulk. Remember the file only need to touch what needs to be removed.

3. Lower Arch: Looking at the nail from the side, remove any product that is dropping down. Start from outer edge and drive the file back into the groove.

SURFACE SMOOTHING:

4. Repeat preliminary shaping 1-3.

5. Side Walls: Using the file vertically straighten the sidewall, white free edge only, beveling toward the center of the nail.

6.pCuticle: "Sprinkler"- using short feathering strokes and keeping file flat start to detail the cuticle area, starting at the smile line and working around.

7. Nail Body: "Frisbee"– contour nail surface using long arching strokes, from groove towards center of nail plate. Use a "Reverse Frisbee" for opposite side. This action will start at the upper nail body and work down to the smile line.

8. Define Arch Location: Elevate hand to eye level. Keep file flat and pull file towards you, do not lift file from surface. Use a side-to-side rocking motion the bevel.

9. Feather and Bevel: With the hand still elevated angle file slightly down to achieve an even thin convex. Use a

side-to-side rocking motion to bevel. Turn hand around to look down the nail surface and refine as needed.

ELECTRIC FILE FILING PROCEDURE

Use electric file and a fine carbide nail drill bit at 10K to 12K RPM (Round Per Minute).

1. Use the whole-body length of the nail drill bit to straighten up both sides of the artificial nail.

2. Carefully smooth out the top 1/4 of the nail (the cuticle area). Aim to taper the product at the cuticle. Create a hair line of groove separating the product from the cuticle (at this step you can

lower the e-file speed to 6K or 8K RPM to avoid injuring client).

3. Using vertical strokes to shave down and smooth out the left part and the right part of the acrylic nail.

4. From side to side and from top to bottom, use the whole length of the drill bit to gently smooth out the entire nail.

5. Buff nail with a buffer block. Dust.

FINISH CRITIQUES FOR ARTIFICIAL ENHANCEMENTS

These guidelines give technicians information on what you should be looking for in a properly built nail. These guidelines will help the technician achieve strong and durable nails with a beautiful look.

C-CURVE (the degree of curve from lower arch to lower arch. This includes the entire lower arch from free edge to nail groove):

•Degree of c-curve
•Concave/Convex
•Feather and Bevel

SMILE LINE (the defining line between the free edge and the nail body extending from nail groove to nail groove to nail groove in a semi "oval V" shape):

•Shape too round/too "V"
•Sharpness
•Smoothness
•Points

TIP FIT (this incorporates the application of the tip to the natural nail):

•Angle

•Straight
•Against Natural Nail
•Tip- too big or small
•Tip- too much resin

GROOVE WALLS (the groove in which the natural nail and the skin connect):

•Straight
•Smooth
•Free of excess product
•Needs to be pinched

ARCH (The highest point on the nail):

•Location
•Transition
• Degree of height

LOWER ARCH (the free edge extending out from the nail groove):
•Drops down
•Pulls up
•Notched with file

CUTICLE AREA (the area at the back of the nail plate where the natural nail grows from the matrix):

•Uneven application of product
•Ledge of product
•Cuts from file
•Needs product

PRODUCT CONTROL (proper use of product):

•Too wet / dry

•Bubbles
•Marbled
SURFACE SMOOTHNESS (overall surface shape):

•File graduation

BALANCE (the overall shape and length of the nail):

•Too long
•Too short
•Check shape

Natural Nail Prep:

Step #1 - Sanitize your hands and your client's hands.

Step #2 - Remove old product from the nails if necessary.

Step #3 - Perform a dry manicure by gently pushing back the cuticle, removing the non-living tissue and shape the nail.

Step #4 - Remove the shine from the nail using a Fine Paper Sanding Band at 4K RPM. Remove the dust from the nail.

Step #5 - Apply 2 coats of Nail Prep Solution or Dehydrator - allow to dry between applications.

Nail-Tip Extensions:

Step #6 - Apply nail glue at the contact point of the tip and slide tip onto nail plate.

Step #7 - Cut tips to desired length.

Step #8 - Gently shape the tips using a 100/100 grit nail file.

Step #9 - Apply 2 coats of Primer – sparingly on the nail plate, allow to dry between each coat and avoid contact with the surrounding skin.

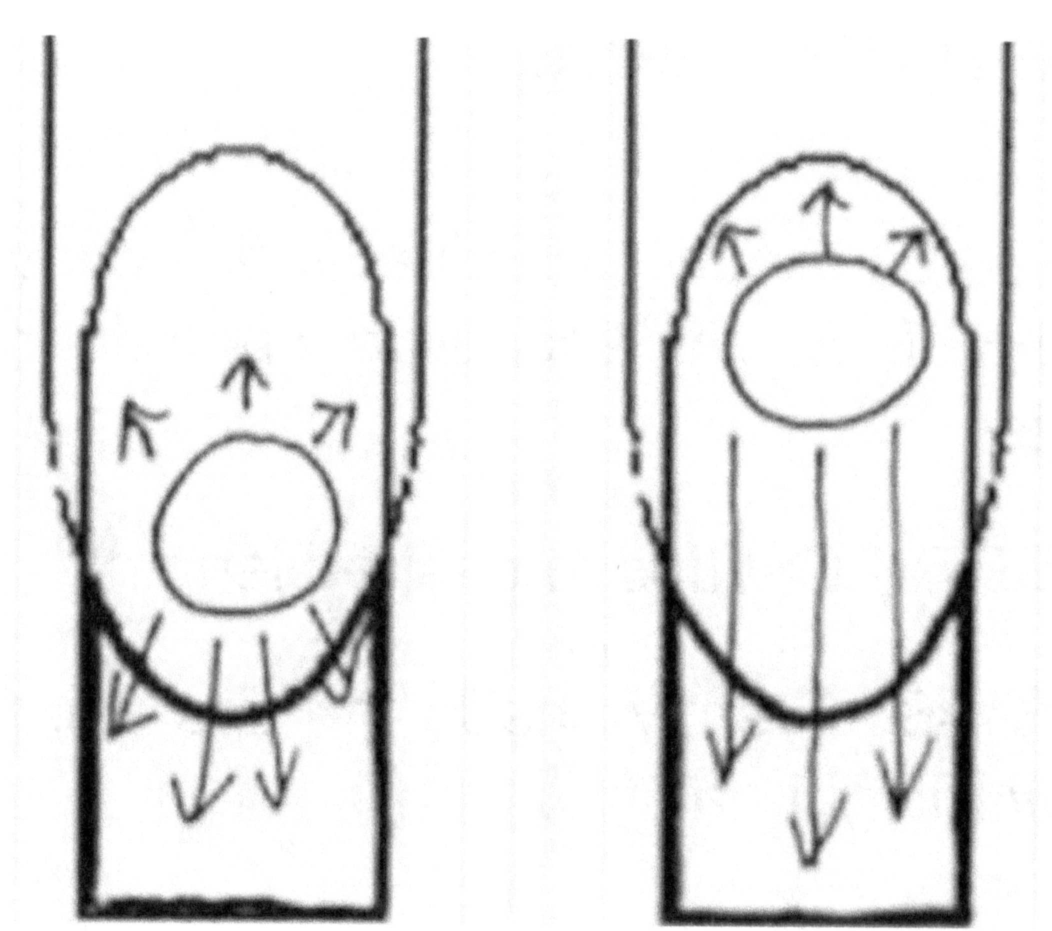

After Completion of All Filing Procedures:

Step #1 - Wash hands (no soap) and scrub with manicure brush. Dry with towel.

Step #2 - Apply LED/UV No-Cleanse Top Gel to the nail and cure 1.5 minutes in LED/UV gel lamp.

Step #3 - Apply Cuticle Oil to moisturize.có

WHITE FRENCH TIP WITH ACRYLIC OVERLAY

Product Application (Clear Powder Only Application):

Step #1 - Ball 1:

•Dip brush in liquid and wipe excess liquid on side of dappen dish. Place tip of brush in Clear Powder until a medium ball of powder final   to the tip of the brush.

•Place this ball of Clear Powder in the center of the nail. Begin working product by pressing the product up to the cuticle then lightly stroke forward towards the free edge.

Step #2 - Ball 2:

•Repeat step 1 to achieve desired shape and structure.

NOTE: Place this ball at the arch location, repeat the pressing application up to the cuticle area and then stroke forward towards the free edge.

NATURAL TIP WITH ACRYLIC OVERLAY

Product Application:

Step #1 - Ball 1: Nail Bed & Free edge:

•Dip brush in liquid and wipe excess liquid on side of dappen dish. Place tip of brush in center of Clear Powder, hold brush until a medium ball of powder adheres to the tip of the brush.

•Place this ball of Clear Powder on natural nail bed, press product up to the cuticle using flat side of brush and stroke forward to move product towards free edge. Wipe brush on paper towel.

Step #2 - Ball 2:

•Repeat step 1 to achieve desired shape and structure.

NOTE: Place this ball at the arch location, repeat the pressing application up to the cuticle area then stroke towards the free edge.

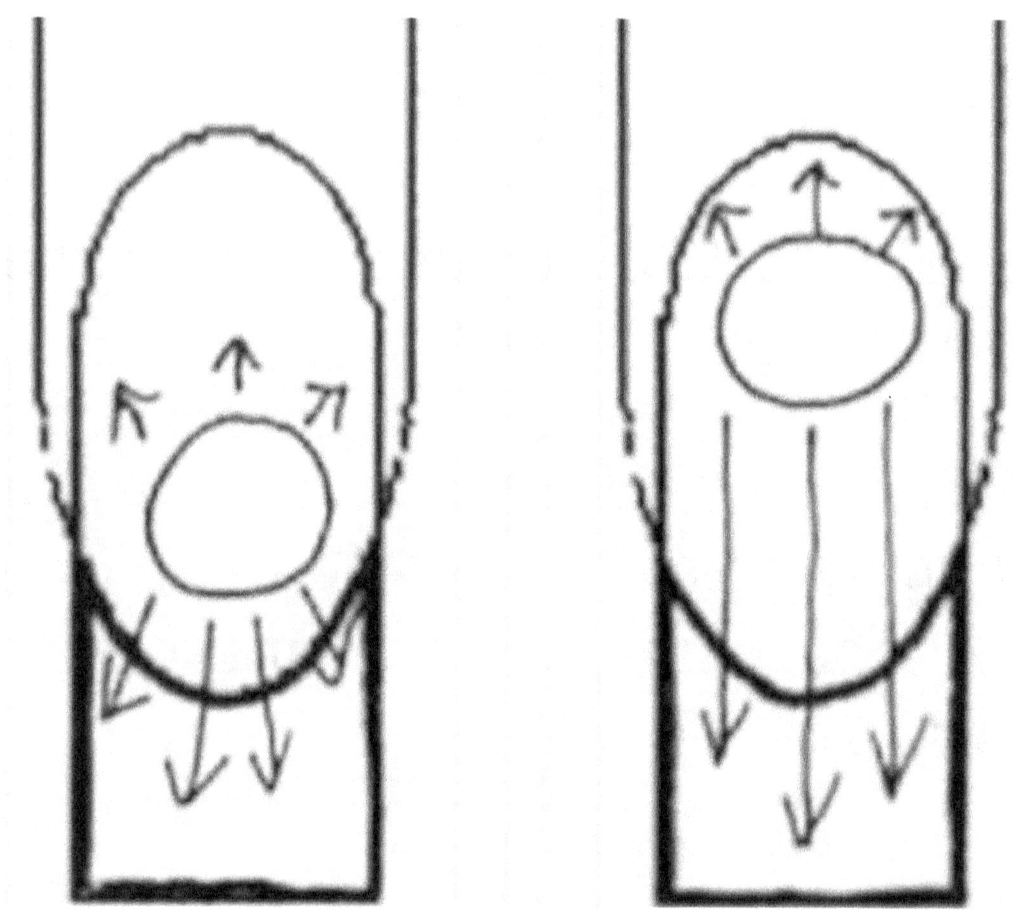

TIP OVERLAY WITH PINK & WHITE ACRYLIC

Step #1 - Ball 1: Free Edge

•1A - Dip brush in liquid and wipe excess liquid on side of dappen dish. Place tip of brush into White Powder until a medium ball of powder adheres to the tip of the brush.

•1B - Place this ball of White Powder on the tip in front of natural nail free edge, shape and form with flat side of brush. Keep mixture within the natural nail line, extending straight out from each nail groove. Wipe brush on paper towel prior to dipping back into the liquid. Refine smile line with tip of brush. Repeat using

White Powder until desired shape and length is created.

NOTE:

•You can also use a French Trimmer (the White Trimmer) or the larger end of a plastic nail tip to carve out the smile line. Use a French brush with some monomer to clean up the white powder residue on the nail bed prior to the pink powder application.

•For the reverse method, apply pink powder from the cuticle area down to at least 4/5 of the nail length. Then use a pink trimmer to cut the pink powder part and create the smile line. Fill the tip area with white powder.

Step #2: Nail Bed

•2A - Ball 2: Dip brush in liquid and wipe excess liquid on side of dappen dish. Place tip of brush in Pink Powder until a medium ball of powder adheres to the tip of the brush. Place this ball of Pink Powder in center of the nail bed and press product up to the cuticle and smile line using flat side of brush and stroke forward towards the free edge. Make sure to keep acrylic off cuticle and skin surrounding the nail. Wipe brush on paper towel.

•2B - Ball 3: Repeat step 2A to achieve desired shape and structure.

NOTE: Place this ball at the arch location, repeat the pressing application up to the cuticle and then stroke forward towards the free edge.

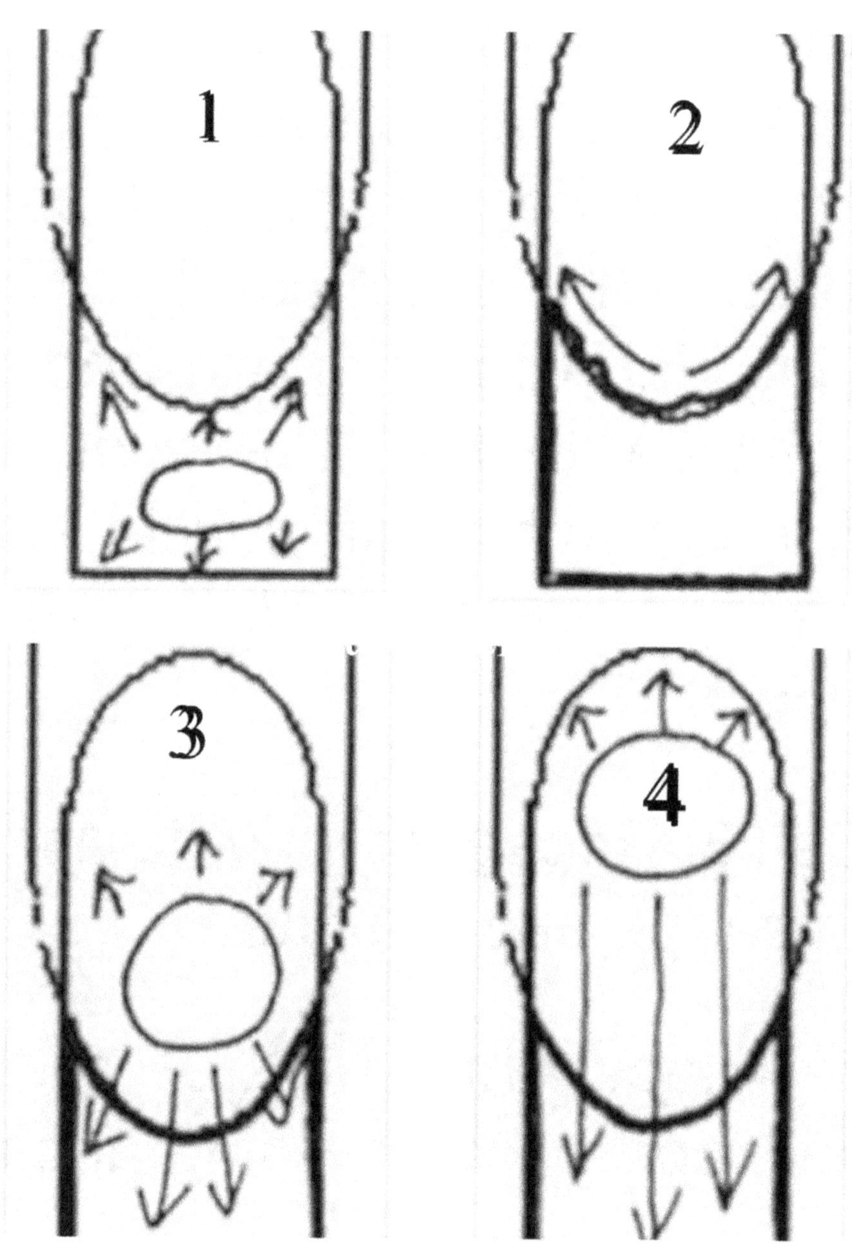

OMBRE AND MARBLED ACRYLIC NAIL ART

•A good balance between the two ombre colors is 1:1 (50/50).

•When creating ombre nails with acrylic powders: Choose colors that are closer to each other. Always using the lighter color for the tip area (zones 2 & 1). For the cover powder (zone 3), make sure to pick an opaque color for good coverage - do not use a sheer color. These are great ombre color pairs: Pink & White; Nude & White; Orange & Yellow; Dark Green & Light Green; Dark Pink & Light Pink; Nude & Light Brown.

•When creating ombre acrylic nail with the "Brushing-On" method: use colors that are further and more contrast to each other. You can use a light color as foundation and use a darker color for the tip area (zones 1 & 2).

•The "Brushing-On" Ombre Method: Create solid color acrylic or dipping acrylic nails. File and buff smooth. Remove dust. Apply a LED/UV Base Gel. Cure for 20 seconds in LED/UV gel lamp. Dip or pour clear acrylic powder to cover the entire nails. Do not dust. Use an ombre nail art brush or a small make-up brush to gradually brush a darker color onto the nail to create the ombre effect. Dust. Seal with LED/UV No-Cleanse Gel Top. Cure.

•For Marble Nails: the more contrast to one another the colors, the more visible the marble effect. Always pick up the lightest color prior to dipping into darker color(s). Use wetter balls of acrylic for easier flow when marbleizing. Be creative and have fun!

•Always encapsulate ombre and/or marble nails with clear powder prior to filing and buffing.

NOTE: For a comprehensive acrylic nail art training course, please visit my website at:

www.pensight.com/x/lona

FRENCH OMBRE ACRYLIC APPLICATION

Step #1:

•1A - Apply White acrylic powder to cover 2/3 of the nail from the free edge. Aim for a thin, even application.

•1B - Apply Pink or Nude Cover powder 1 hair line away from the cuticle and using feather strokes to blend it down and cover 1/3 of the white powder.

Step #2:

Encapsulate the whole nail in a thin layer of Clear acrylic powder.

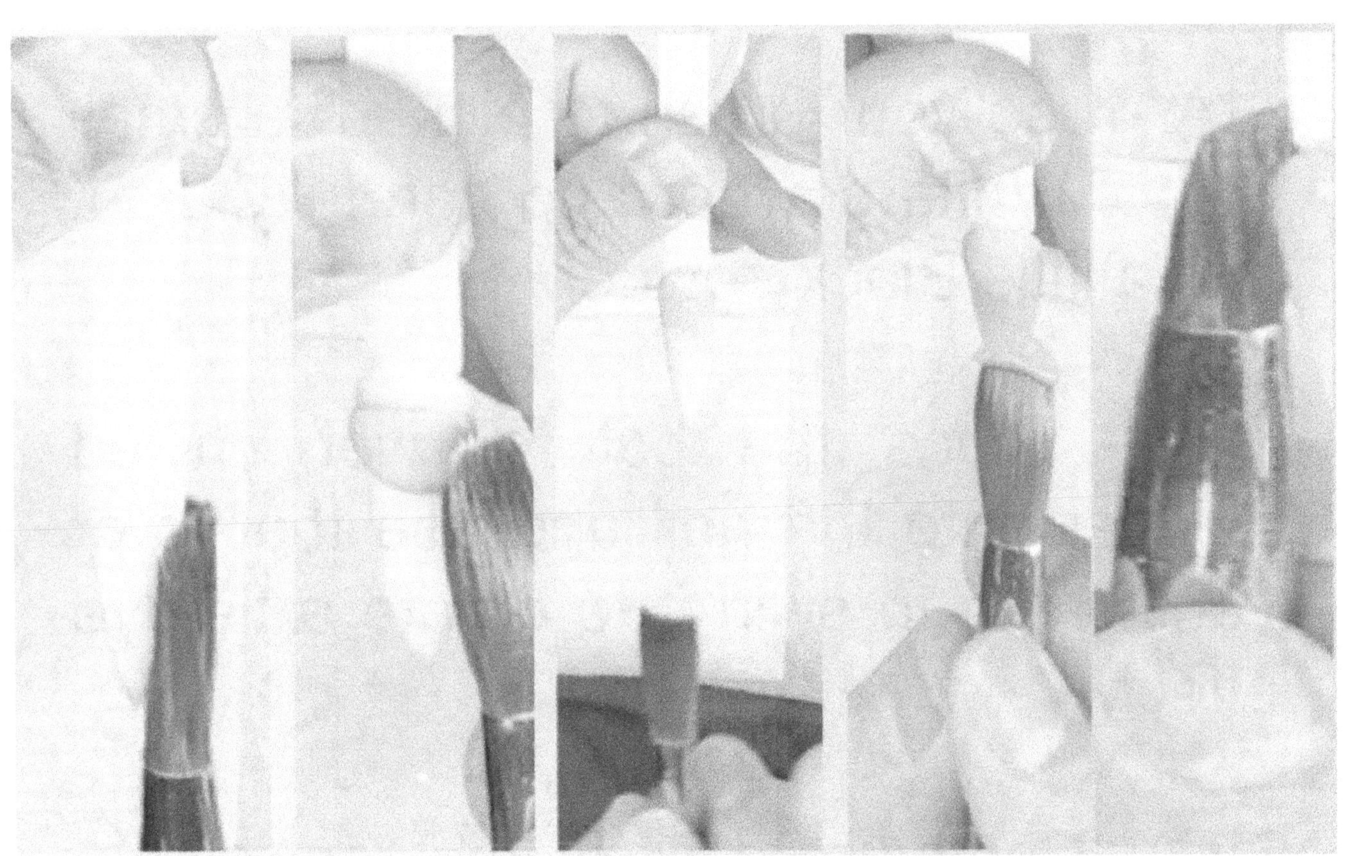

BLACK & WHITE MARBLED ACRYLIC APPLICATION

Step #1:

•1A - Use your brush to pick up a small ball of White powder and carefully dip it into a little Black powder.

•1B - Place the ball of wet, mixed powder onto the nail and use the tip of your brush to swirl it to create a tie-dye effect.

•1C - Continue to fill in the rest of the nail surface with various sized of wet, mixed powder balls.

Step #2:

Encapsulate the whole nail in a thick layer of clear powder to create a proper nail structure.

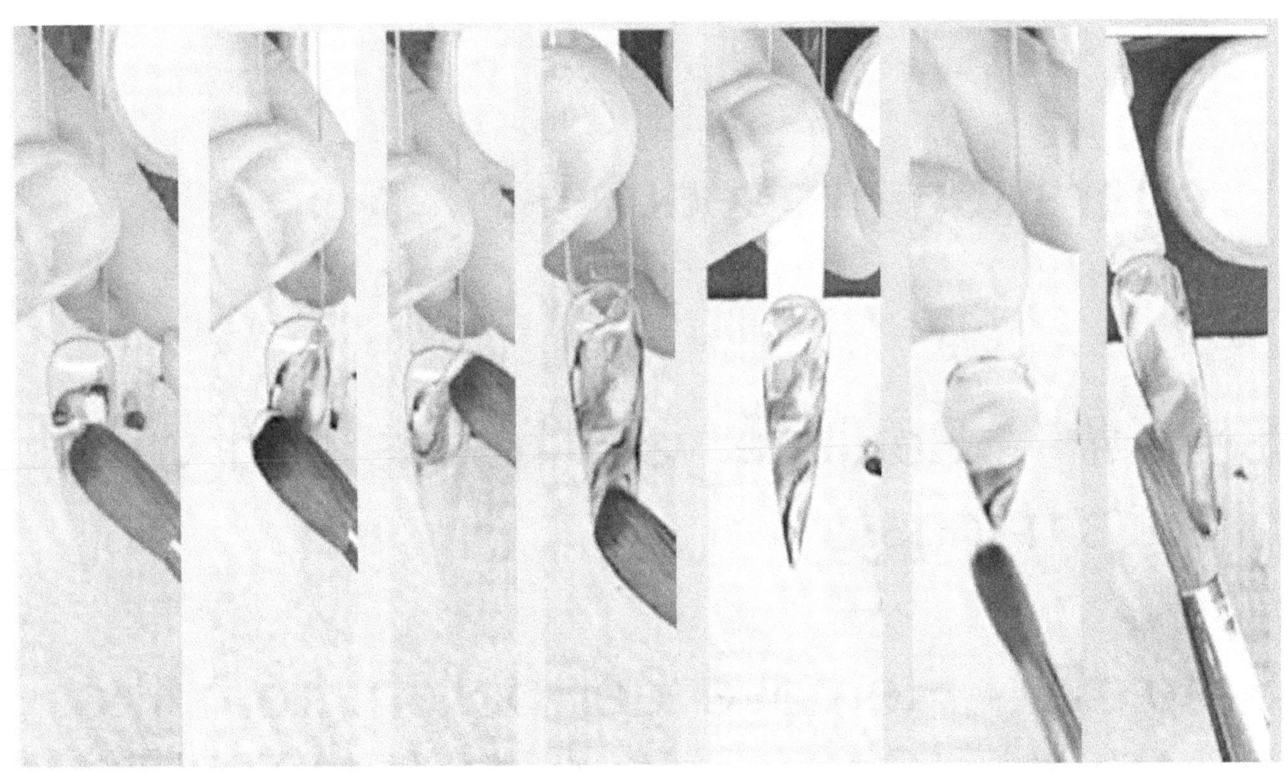

This maintenance (acrylic fill-in service) should be done every 2 to 3 weeks.

Preparation Procedures:

Step #1 - Sanitize your hands and your client's hands.

Step #2 - Remove gel polish from the nails with a Coarse Carbide Nail Drill Bit at 12K RPM if necessary.

Step #3 - Perform a dry manicure by gently pushing back the cuticle, removing the non-living tissue and shape the nail.

Step #4 - Smooth out the acrylic product at the growing area (zone 3) using a Medium Carbide Nail Drilled Bit at 8K to 10K RPM. Using a Fine Paper Sanding Band at 6K RPM, blend artificial surface to the natural nail and also remove all dead tissues at the growing area. Remove excess length and shape free edge with 100 Grit Nail File. Remove dust from the nail.

Step #5 - Apply 2 coats of Dehydrator – allow it to dry between applications.

Step #6 - Apply 2 coats of Nail Primer – sparingly on the nail plate, allow it to dry between each coat and be sure avoid contact to the surrounding skin.

Step #7 - Ball 1: Dip brush in liquid and wipe excess liquid on side of dappen dish. Place tip of brush in center of the Pink or Clear Powder or Powder of the same color as the acrylic nail until a small ball of powder adheres to the tip of the brush (about the size of a small pea). Place this ball of powder on natural nail bed (behind the artificial nail) and press product using flat side of brush up to the cuticle. Stroke forward to blend with nail surface all the way over the free edge. Wipe brush on towel.

Step #8 - Ball 2: Add a small wet ball of powder to perfect the cuticle area. Wipe brush on towel.

Finishing The Nail:

Step #9 - Following steps in Filing Techniques (page 50 to page 55).

Step #10 - Wash hands (no soap) and scrub with manicure brush. Dry with towel.

Step #11 - Apply 2 to 3 coats of color gel polish if necessary - curing each layer 1.5 minutes.

Step #11 - Apply LED/UV No-Wipe Gel Top Coat and cure for 1.5 minutes in LED/UV gel lamp.

Step #12 - Apply Cuticle Oil to moisturize.

ACRYLIC TOO RUNNY:

Room temperature too low (under 72*F) or too much liquid in acrylic nail brush. Clear powder and some glitter powders also tend to be runnier, so after picking up a ball of acrylic, dap the other side of your brush on paper towel to release excess liquid.

ACRYLIC DRIES TOO QUICKLY:

Room temperature too high (above 78*F). Not enough liquid in brush. MMA liquid will cause acrylic powder to polymerize much quicker than EMA liquid.

UNEVEN CUTICLE APPLICATION:

Use a 3-ball application method. Apply the first ball of acrylic (large ball) to cover 2/3 of the nail length from the free edge (from zone 2 down to zone 1 of nail length). Apply the second ball (medium ball) to cover the remaining area (zone 3 - cuticle area) but stay away about 1mm from the cuticle. Apply the third ball (small, wet ball) at the cuticle area, and when the powder is still runny, use the tip of your brush to round off the powder contouring with the curve shape of the cuticle.

FRENCH DIPPING NATURAL NAIL OVERLAY

STEP #1 - Pour White dipping powder into a disposable dipping tray.

STEP #2 - Apply 1 coat of Prep Solution #1 to each finger and allow it to dry.

*If extending the nail with nail tips, follow the tip application technique, then proceed to the following step.

STEP #3— Apply a coat of Dip Base #2 to the entire nail of the pinky of one hand and carefully slide finger forward into the white powder to create a crisp smile line.

STEP #4 - Immediately dip entire finger into the pink or clear dipping powder in the container and tap off excess.

STEP #5 - Repeat the above step on the other four nails of the same hand.

STEP #6 - Gently dust off excess powder with a clean nail dust brush. Apply a generous amount of Activator #3 to all five nails, making sure to cap the free edges.

STEP #7 - Repeat the dipping process on the five nails of the other hand - making sure your smile lines are crisp. Then loosely close the Dip Base #2 bottle cap.

STEP #8— Gently dust off excess powder.

STEP #9— Apply a generous amount of Activator #3 to all five nails, making sure to cap the free edge.

STEP #10— File and shape all nails with a 100-grit nail file. Smooth out the nail surface with a fine carbide bit at 8K RPM, then buff smooth.

STEP #11— Remove dust from all nails, making sure no dust particles are left on the nails.

STEP #12— Re-apply the Activator #3 on all ten nails.

STEP #13 - IMPORTANT: Without pausing between fingers, apply a coat of the Glue Top #4 to one hand only and immediately apply a second coat of Glue Top #4 to that same hand. Do not over brush the second coat, limit to three strokes per nail.

STEP #14 - Repeat the above step on the other hand.

STEP #15— Let the Glue Top #4 dry for 5 minutes before applying cuticle oil.

*STEP #12 - Alternative Application: Apply a thin coat of LED/UV No-Cleanse Gel Top Coat to one hand, making sure to cap the free edge. Place hand in LED or UV lamp and cure 90 seconds in LED/UV gel lamp, there is no need to cleanse the nails afterwards. Repeat on the other hand. Apply cuticle oil.

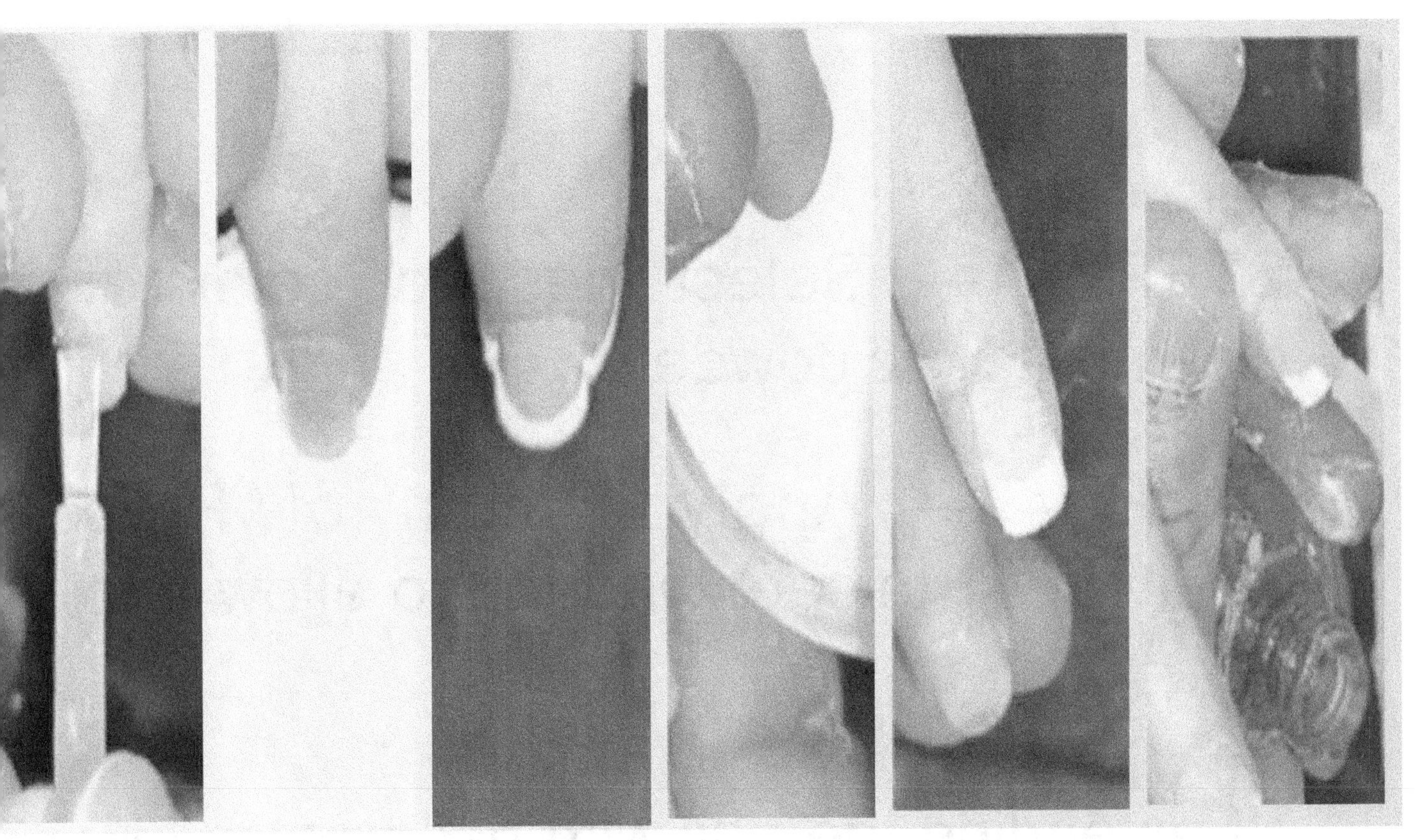

STEP #1— Select desired color of dipping acrylic powder.

STEP #2— Apply 1 coat of Prep Solution #1 to each finger and allow it to dry.

*If extending the nail with nail tips, follow the tip application technique, then proceed to the following step.

STEP #3 - Apply a coat of Glue Base #2 to the pinky of one hand and carefully slide finger forward into the color powder making sure to cover the entire nail bed and tap off excess powder.

STEP #4— Repeat the above step on all nails of the same hand.

STEP #5— Gently dust off excess powder from nails with a clean nail dust brush.

STEP #6— Repeat the dipping process (STEP #3) on all five nails of that hand for a second layer of color powder, making sure to evenly cover the entire nail bed, then loosely close the Glue Base #2 bottle cap.

STEP #7— Gently dust off excess powder from nails.

STEP #8— Apply a generous amount of Activator #3 to all five nails making sure to cap the free edge.

STEP #9—Repeat STEP #3 to STEP #8 for nails of the other hand.

STEP #10— Starting with the first hand, file and shape all nails with a 100-grit nail file, smooth out the nail surface with a fine carbide bit at 8K RPM, and buff smooth.

*To seal the nails, follow step 11 to step 15 of the last procedure (French Dipping Nails).

DIPPING ACRYLIC TROUBLESHOOTING

•Dip powder is not sticking to the base – Not enough base, brush on a slightly thicker amount of base and dip the finger into dip powder immediately.

•Activator #3 brush stiffening – Not cleaning Activator #3 brush properly, make sure to completely dust off any remains of dip powder before brushing on Activator #3 and wipe off brush on a clean paper towel.

•Glue Top #4 not shiny – Not dusting off nail surface properly or applying it too slowly. Make sure to only apply to 5 nails at a time and apply two coats.

BRUSH FERRULE: The metal band at the end of the brush handle that houses the bristles.

BRUSH TIP: The furthest finest hairs found at the end of the brush, great for detail and precise applications.

CURVE: The degree of curve from nail groove to nail groove.

CONCAVE: The underneath portion of the free-edge rim.

CONVEX: The top side of the free edge rim.

COVALENT: Permanent chemical bonds that join one unit.

CURE: Activating the photo initiator in order to set the gel.

CUTICLE: The dead tissue which tightly adheres to the natural nail plate.

DISINFECTION: Kills all pathogens on a surface, and is almost as effective as sterilization

DRY ROUGH SURFACE: Removing nail shine and any oil or residue from the nail plate with a fine paper sanding band.

EPONYCHIUM: The living tissue at the base of the nail covering the matrix.

EPOXY RESIN: The adhesive used to hold the brush bristles in place inside the ferrule.

FLASH CURE: The process to stop the movement of the gel, 10-30 seconds.

FORWARD/DOWN: Towards the free-edge.

FREE-EDGE: The extension of the nail plate over the tip of the finger.

HYPONYCHIUM: The living tissue under the free-edge of the nail that completes the seal between the two lateral folds, protecting the nail bed.

LOWER ARCH: The bottom edge of the sidewall, extending parallel from the nail groove.

LUNULA: The whitish area of the nail plate located 1at the base of the nail near or under the eponychium. The shape of the free-edge is directly related to the shape of the lunula.

MATRIX: Area where the nail plate cells are formed. The area is composed of matrix cells that make up the nail plate.

NAIL GROOVE: Slits or tracks at either side of the nail upon which the nail moves as it grows.

NON-LIVING TISSUE: The dead tissue found on the nail plate that must be removed prior to artificial nail application.

OLIGOMER: A partially polymerized polymer or a few molecules of gel already linked together.

OVEREXPOSURE: A chemical hazard caused by prolonged and/or repeated exposure beyond accepted safe levels.

PHOTO-INITIATORS: A chemical catalyst activated by UV light.

PITTING: Pits or holes in the body of the artificial nail.

SANITATION: Greatly reduces the number of pathogens or bacteria on a surface.

SHRINKAGE: Nail product pulling away from the edges during the curing process.

SIDEWALL: The extension of the artificial nail from the nail groove. It defines the sides of the free-edge.

SMILE LINE: A gentle arch from sidewall to sidewall located at the edge of the nail bed.

SPIKING: Sharp peaks/spikes on the artificial nail surface.

STERILIZATION: Completely destroys all living organisms on an object or surface, including spores.

PRIMER DON'TS:

When using Primer, avoid contact with artificial tips and product. Primer may cause tips to shatter and/or yellow. Overexposing the skin to primer, may cause skin irritation and burning. Neutralize the skin with Dehydrator.

PREPARATION OF THE WHITE FRENCH NAIL TIP:

The White French Nail Tip was designed to give you the "Perfect" smile line. When removing the surface shine, be sure not to file into the smile line. File in the direction from the free-edge towards the cuticle, not downward. This will prevent you from filing, nicking or blending the smile line.

CLEANING YOUR ACRYLIC BRUSH:

Frequently dip your brush into EMA monomer and wipe it on a clean paper towel to remove acrylic residue. Soak your brush in a brush cleaner solution or EMA monomer for maintenance. Do not soak or clean the brush in Acetone!

BRUSH STORAGE:

Always clean and store gel brushes in a DARK, LINT & DUST FREE area

(Example: A travel toothbrush holder or pencil case). Avoid placing in the path of any UV lamp, interior and exterior lighting.

ADDITIONAL BRUSHES:

It is recommended to have more than one acrylic brush to accomplish several procedures. Designating a brush for different procedures eliminates the possibility of having unwanted pigment or glitter.

SPIKING:

Spiking (heat spike) is caused by having a contaminated artificial nail surface and/ or to rapid of curing a large amount of gel product.   After finishing filing, cleansing the nail surface with Alcohol or washing hands without soap before applying a top coat may help prevent surface spiking. To prevent curing too rapidly when using gel, place the hand in the gel lamp palm up for the first 10-15 seconds of the cure then turn over for the recommended cure time.

UV LIGHT HEAT SENSITIVITY:

Heat sensitivity is caused by the friction of the molecular activity once in contact with an UV light. Clients may be more prone to having heat sensitivity for the following reasons: thin nail beds, thick product application or clients nearing menstruation. If heat is felt at any time, pull hand out of the UV light and wait for the nail to cool and continue to cure the remaining time. The following tips may be used to prevent heat sensitivity:

•Place the hand in front of the light for 2-3 seconds, allowing the UV light to slowly activate the molecules.

•Gradually move the hand into the light every 2-3 seconds until fully placed in the UV Lamp.

•Place the hand upside down into the UV lamp for 10-15 seconds, allowing the indirect light to cure the gel slowly. Then turn the hand over and place inside the UV Lamp and cure for the recommended cure time.

THUMB CURING:

"Uncured" or "pooling" product on the thumb is caused when the thumb is turned down towards the bottom of the UV Lamp. To prevent this, apply the gel to the thumbs separately and cure alone facing the nail bed straight up towards the bulbs and cure. Repeat if second coat is desired.

GELS PEEL/LIFT:

Gel on surrounding skin or cuticles will cause lifting. Check UV Bulbs, remember UV Bulbs do not burn out but they do lose their strength. You should change them every 6 months if using daily or once a year if not using lamp often.

NATURAL NAIL OVERLAY EDGE CHIPPING and/or SEPARATING:

When the nail is short, it is hard to completely surround the free-edge, causing the product to chip and/or separate on the free edge. Slightly lengthening an overlay on a nail form will allow the whole free-edge to be completely capped with product. Cure the recommended time, remove form, cleanse and proceed with shaping the nail.

GEL POLISH NOT CURING:

Some gel polish colors are pigmented very heavily, causing them to not cure in the recommended time. To ensure a full cure, apply these colors in thin coats, curing for 2 minutes between coats.

BUBBLE IN FINISHED NAILS:

Make sure to control the ratio of acrylic and monomer - not having enough monomer in your brush while picking up acrylic powder will create air pockets within the product. Do not overwork acrylic or gel. Do not pat gel polish like an acrylic. Apply gel polish with light-pressure and long strokes. DO NOT STIR gel polish with the bottle brush before using - shake the whole gel bottle by rolling it in the palms of your hands.

ACRYLIC TOO DRY OR TOO RUNNY:

Monomer (acrylic liquid) is very sensitive to working room temperature. The ideal room temperature to work with EMA monomer is between 72*F to 76*F. By placing the monomer container in a bowl of either cold or hot water will help you adjust the consistency of the acrylic application.

WHITE ACRYLIC/GEL DISCOLORED OR YELLOW:

Sun beds, tanning products, smoking and hair color could cause staining. Keep nails away from the above products. Wear rubber gloves.

REPAIRING A CHIPPED NAIL:

If a client has a chip on the free-edge of her nail, it can be fixed without replacing it. Simply prep the nail as you would for a regular service. Place a form on the nail, and build out the chipped area on the form.

REPAIRING A LIFTED NAIL:

When repairing a nail that has lifted, make sure all of the lifted area has been removed by filing… do not nip or cut Nipping and cutting will only break the seal further, and be more difficult to file flush again. Gently file the lifted area, until it is flush with the nail. This way you will have no visible fill line in your finished nail. If the glue on the tip has lifted from the nail, remove the tip and replace if necessary.

RESTORING THE SHINE ON A DULL GEL NAIL:

Using a fine paper sanding band at 8K RPM, remove the shine from the entire nail and remove any dust. Apply LED/UV No-Wipe Top Gel to the nail and cure.

CLIENT RETURNS FOR A FILL WITH A CRACKED NAIL:

Determine whether the crack is only in the product or is through the nail itself. If it's only in the product, file the nail down to the point of the crack, and rebalance the nail as normal. Make sure to reinforce the area, to make up for the excess product removed. Remove any dust filings. Continue throughout the remaining steps of the nail. If the crack is through the natural nail, do not fill. File to remove the product in the area and check for any signs of infection or bleeding. Have the client wait until the area heals, or refer them to a physician. If the area looks healthy, you can proceed in re-applying product. Make sure you reinforce the area to prevent any future stress.

BREAKING NAILS:

•Is there enough acrylic in the stress area? If not, build the area up, by adding more acrylic at the stress area (at about 2/3 of the natural nail bed, under the cuticle area). Be sure to maintain the Apex while filing the nail.

•Is the nail breaking in the area where the tip is glued to the nail? Is the glue separating from the tip, and placing stress on the nail? Is the product separating from the nail? Make sure you are using a quality nail adhesive to apply the tip and that you have complete adhesion before moving onto application of product. Also, make sure you have enough product on the stress area of the nail to accommodate the client's life style and nail length. Also, pay close attention to the primer application. Do not get primer on the tip as it can weaken the tip.

•Is there an air pocket in the area of the break? File open the air pocket; blend the edges so no lines are visible. Re-apply product.

BUMPY GEL POLISH SURFACE:

Gel application is too thick. Apply gel polish in thinner layers. Allow gel polish to "float" (to self-level) by pointing the nails up for a few seconds before placing the hand in the gel lamp.

LIFTING NAILS:

•Is there none-living tissue on the nail plate? If so, remove and reapply product.

•Is the client on any medications? Medications change the body's chemistry, and therefore the chemical balance in the nail plate. Antibiotics and many other medications can cause havoc on a client who regularly has no problems with her nails. Pregnancy can also cause sudden lifting on a client who previously has had no such problems.

•Do you live in a very dry climate, or very humid climate? You may find it necessary to use 3 coats of acrylic primer. Weather conditions can greatly influence body's chemistry and contribute to lifting or bonding issues with nail products.

•Experiment, and diagnose. We learn by trial and error on some clients. If you need to narrow something down, try doing one method on one hand and another method on the other hand. Just remember to record what you've done, so you remember what works! Also make sure they are choosing a style and length of nail that is appropriate to their lifestyle. Extensions that are too long for the length of the natural nail bed can cause lifting. The nail is out of balance. Consult with your client for a nail length that is more appropriate for them. Use cuticle pusher or orange wood stick to remove any product that may have gotten on the cuticles before curing. Product that has cured on the skin will cause lifting.

SKIN IRRITATION VS. ALLERGIC REACTION:

•Skin Irritation: Harsh chemicals that come in contact with the skin can cause skin irritation. These harsh chemicals include but are not limited to acetone, methacrylic acid, primers, strong polish removers, formaldehyde, etc. Avoid skin contact as much as possible and follow the directions on the product label. The typical symptoms of skin irritation are dry skin, mild burning, mild itching, redness and possibly some mild cracking such as you would experience with hands that are chapped by water. Removing the product from its contact with the skin will usually immediately eliminate or reduce the symptoms.

•Allergic Reaction: Repeated skin exposures/irritation to harsh chemicals that, over time, cause the body to develop antibodies causing a allergic reaction - allergic contact dermatitis (ACD). When a foreign chemical gets into the blood stream and activates the body's immune system, the body will respond to the foreign chemical by producing antibodies. These antibodies attack the foreign chemical by producing antibodies. These antibodies attack the foreign chemical in an attempt to destroy or neutralize it. Allergic reactions typically develop over time and do not appear after the first time a product is used. Symptoms of an allergic reaction to a substance will typically appear within 24 - 48 hours of exposure to the substance. The typical symptoms of a mild allergic reaction, especially the more intense swelling and itching should allow you to tell it apart from skin irritation. Severe allergic reactions can include: severe swelling of the finger or hand, (including the arm, face or eyes), severe itching and burning, cracking and bleeding skin, lifting of the natural nail plate, etc. If the client or nail technician experiences any allergic reactions, the product should be immediately removed and the client should see their physician as soon as possible. Severe reactions should be treated immediately. The client should stop using the product. Prevent allergic reactions from developing by eliminating the product from having contact or exposure to the skin. Keep all products off your skin and your client's skin, avoid areas that are cut or open and wash your hands and have the clients wash their hands thoroughly with soap and water after every service.

ACCELERATED ONLINE NAIL TRAINING COURSES & BOOKS AT:

www.pensight.com/x/lona

CONCLUSION

I hope you enjoy my book and that it serves you well in your nail endeavors! I know some aspects of it can seem complicated, but trust the process, practice your skills, and soon you will become an accomplished nail professional.

Happy doing nails!

Andy Hai Dinh

For accelerated online nail training courses, nail related materials, and nail related Q&As, please visit:

www.pensight.com/x/lona

For hand-picked nail tools and nail accessories, please visit:

www.shoplona.company.site

LIFE OF NAIL ACADEMY

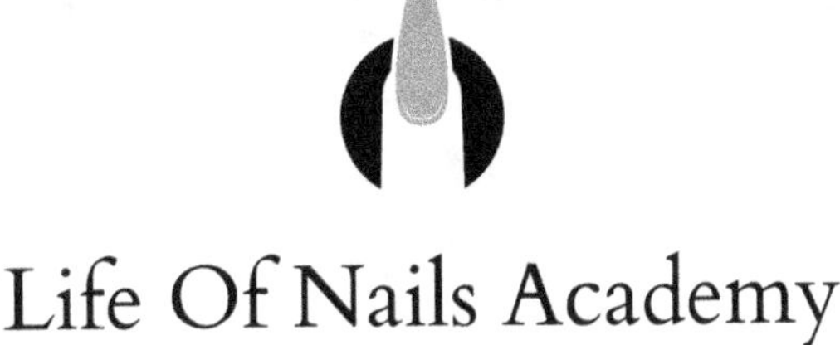

Life Of Nails Academy

Nail Your Future!

BOOKS BY THIS AUTHOR:

•*Acrylic and Dipping Powder: Product Knowledge and Applications*
(publication year: 2023)

•*The Nail technician's Career Guide: The Blueprint to A Successful Nail Salon Business*
(publication year: 2023)

•*A Beginner's Guide to Trading: Stock and Forex Technical Analysis*
(publication year: 2025)

•*WIN MORE, TRADE BETTER: A Practical Guide to Trading and Investing*
(publication year: 2025)

•*Modern Vietnamese Cuisine: The Best Home- Cooking Recipes*
(publication year: 2025)

•*Modern Vietnamese Cuisine 2: Family Meals for All Occasions*
(publication year: 2025)

Watch for more at
www.pensight.com/x/lona